NAKUPENDA

nah-koo-pen-dah

means

I LOVE YOU

BUT..
WHAT IS SWAHILI FOR LOVE?

IT IS NOT

♥ **Mambo** ♥

mam-boh

WHICH MEANS
WHAT'S UP?

OR

♥ **Jambo** ♥

Jam-boh

WHICH MEANS

HELLO

NOR

Haraka
ha-rah-kah

WHICH MEANS FASTER

NEITHER

♥ **Polepole** ♥

poh-leh-poh-leh-

AND

NAKUPENDA

nah-koo-pen-dah

means

I LOVE YOU

so
WHAT IS SWAHILI FOR LOVE?

IT IS NOT
♥ Cheka ♥
nee-nee

WHICH MEANS

LAUGH

OR

♥ Lia ♥

lee-ah

WHICH MEANS **SING**

N OR

❤ Sikiliza ❤

see-key-lee-zah

I KNOW
NAKUPENDA
nah-koo-pen-dah

means

I LOVE YOU

SO...
WHAT IS SWAHILI FOR LOVE?

IT IS NOT

♥ Furaha ♥

foo-rah-ha

WHICH MEANS JOY

OR

♥ **Huzuni** ♥

hoo-zoo-nee

NEITHER

Jiji

jee-jee

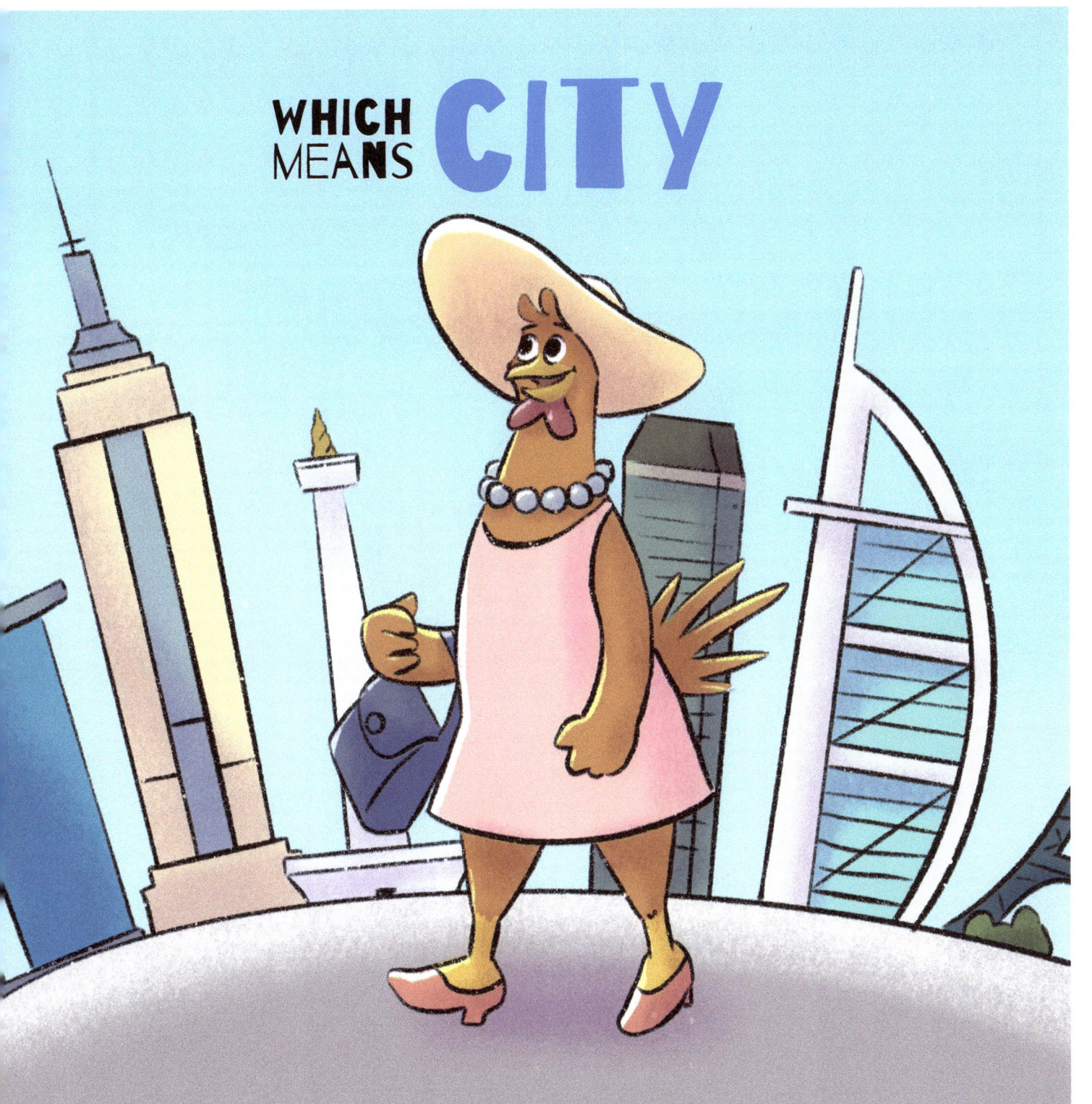

SO...
WHAT IS SWAHILI FOR LOVE?

IT IS NOT
Kelele
keh-leh-leh

OR

Kimya

keym-yah

WHICH MEANS QUIET

SO...
WHAT IS SWAHILI FOR LOVE?

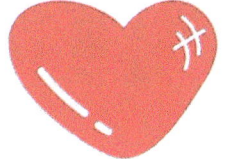

I KNOW IT IS NOT

SO WHAT IS
SWAHILI FOR LOVE?

TURN THE PAGE AND SEE

UPENDO

oo-pen-doh

IS **SWAHILI** FOR LOVE

AND
NAKUPENDA
nah-koo-pen-dah

means

I LOVE YOU

YES I DO

I LOVE YOU

"SASA YANADUMU HAYA MATATU: IMANI, TUMAINI NA UPENDO; LAKINI LILILO KUU KUPITA YOTE NI UPENDO."

"AND NOW THESE THREE REMAIN: FAITH, HOPE AND LOVE. BUT THE GREATEST OF THESE IS LOVE."

FOR HOPE SHIRIRI|GRACE FURAHA|EZRA ELISIFU|ELI SAGAVALA

www.ingramcontent.com/pod-product-compliance
Lightning Source LLC
Chambersburg PA
CBHW061139010526
44107CB00069B/2986